The Lessons Learned Series

Wondering how the most accomplished leaders from around the globe have tackled their toughest challenges? Now you can find out—with Lessons Learned. Concise and engaging, each volume in this new series offers twelve to fourteen insightful essays by top leaders in business, the public sector, and academia on the most pressing issues they've faced.

A crucial resource for today's busy executive, Lessons Learned gives you instant access to the wisdom and expertise of the world's most talented leaders.

Other books in the series:

Leading by Example
Managing Change
Managing Your Career
Managing Conflict
Starting a Business
Hiring and Firing
Making the Sale

Executing
for Results

Executing for Results

LES50NS

Boston, Massachusetts

Library of Congress Cataloging-in-Publication Data
Executing for results.
     p. cm. — (Lessons learned)
  ISBN 978-1-4221-2641-7
 1. Strategic planning. 2. Management.
 HD30.28.E955 2008
 658.4'012—dc22

                               2008005790

In partnership with Fifty Lessons, a leading provider of digital media content,
Harvard Business School Press is pleased to
announce the launch of Lessons Learned,
a new book series that showcases the trusted
voices of the world's most experienced
leaders. Through the power of personal
storytelling, each book in this series pre-
sents the accumulated wisdom of some of
the world's best-known experts and offers
insights into how these individuals think,
approach new challenges, and use hard-won
lessons from experience to shape their leadership philosophies. Organized thematically
according to the topics at the top of managers' agendas—leadership, change management, entrepreneurship, innovation, and
strategy, to name a few—each book draws
from Fifty Lessons' extensive video library
of interviews with CEOs and other thought

A Note from the Publisher

leaders. Here, the world's leading senior executives, academics, and business thinkers speak directly and candidly about their triumphs and defeats. Taken together, these powerful stories offer the advice you'll need to take on tomorrow's challenges.

We invite you to join the conversation now. You'll find both new ways of looking at the world, and the tried-and-true advice you need to illuminate the path forward.

↤ CONTENTS ↦

Contents

Executing
for Results

Strategy Doesn't Compensate for Poor Execution

Ivan Seidenberg

CEO, Verizon

STRATEGY IS AN ISSUE that has evolved in my mind over the last fifteen or twenty years. If you go back fifteen or twenty years, you had to read Michael Porter's work. You had to think about business models and strategic differentiation and strategic advantage and the long-term advantage in your business. And all of that is correct.

What I've learned along the way is, you need to take that plus one very important idea. And that is, the companies that have the best strategies are the companies that execute better than anybody else. Trick shots do not offset weak businesses; strategy does not compensate for poor execution at a business.

One of the things that works is, the better that you develop a culture around execution, the more options you have. What we've learned is, the more market share we take and the more we get ahead of our competition, the more we can do.

Let's take an example of that. If you look at two things going on today—take our wireless business—a lot of people have wireless companies, and a lot of people have wireless licenses. We chose to decide that there is a differentiation that we wanted to create. We didn't want to be a commodity provider; we didn't want to be just a wireless company that was based on cost.

Executing for Results

So one of the things that our marketing, sales, and management teams figured out is the expression, "Can you hear me now?" It was a way to explain to the customer that we understood their requirement. They didn't just want a cool phone that didn't work; they wanted a cool phone that worked really well.

That's an example of strategy being born from great execution—simple things like if you can complete the call, you can then do more things with your network. You can give customers greater products and services. You can create differentiation from your competition. And then you can build the business from that point on.

Another example: we've been in the telecommunications business for a long time. The landline business, the fixed-wire business, was shrinking like crazy. We could milk it, and we could put Band-Aids on it, but what we had that was most important was the direct relationship with our customers. We knew, if we could find a way to take our customers to the next place, we could do really good things in terms of creating growth for our business, our shareholders, and our employees.

We decided to go all nine yards, and we put in a plan to put in fiber optics directly to the home—very ambitious. But this is where solid execution would now create addressable markets that would not have been available to the company had we not focused on the idea of execution first, strategy second.

If there's anything I've learned over the last fifteen to twenty years, [it's] you love strategy. You love to debate it, you love to have all these meetings about strategic intent, and you love to talk about the next ten years. But none of it works if the trains don't run on time. And run better than your competition every day that you get up and go to work.

TAKEAWAYS

- ✒ Traditional strategy holds true today: think about business models, strategic differentiation, strategic advantage, and long-term advantage.

- ✒ Today, you must take that strategy one step further: the companies that have the best strategies are the companies that execute better than anybody else.

- ✒ "Trick shots" do not offset weak businesses, and strategy does not compensate for poor execution.

- ✒ Develop your culture around execution, and then focus on strategy. Doing so creates new opportunities and sets you apart from the competition.

Bridging the Knowing-Doing Gap

Jeffrey Pfeffer

*Thomas D. Dee II Professor of Organizational
Behavior at the Graduate School of Business,
Stanford University*

I WROTE A BOOK CALLED *The Human
Equation: Building Profits by Putting People First* and another book called *Competi-
tive Advantage Through People.* Based on

those two books, I gave enormous numbers of talks about building high-performance work practices and high-performance cultures in companies.

After many of those talks, the following would happen. People would come up to me, and I remember one person very clearly who came up to me after one of these talks. He said, "That was a great talk. I have to tell you two things that I didn't like about it."

I said, "Fine, let me know. I'm always trying to improve."

He said, "First of all, everything you said was common sense."

And I said, "That's probably right, because actually treating people well, letting them be involved in decisions, and providing a certain amount of employment security probably does make, if you think about it, common sense."

He said, "So, first of all, everything was common sense. And second, everything you've told me I already knew."

I said, "That's great. By the way, do you do any of it?"

Executing for Results

The answer, of course, was no.

Having had that one vivid experience and then a bunch of other experiences the same way—where people would say, "We kind of knew this," and I would ask them, "Are you doing it?" and they would say no—it occurred to me that there was just a lot of wisdom and knowledge that people and organizations had that was never being applied.

That got me really interested in why organizations knew things that they didn't then implement. So I found my dear colleague and friend Bob Sutton. He and I went off to explore this phenomenon, and the result was the research that appeared in a book called *The Knowing-Doing Gap: How Smart Companies Turn Knowledge into Action.*

The basic idea behind the book was to discover why organizations would not apply these things—including, by the way, the organization of which I'm a member, Stanford Business School. Stanford Business School is like the king of knowing-doing gaps, where if you were to ask, "Do we apply anything we teach in this business school?" the answer would be no. We teach strategy; we don't have one. We teach human resources; our HR policies are a mess. We teach marketing, but our branding has been completely insufficient and inadequate.

It's fascinating to think about why people would not apply things that they know to their lives and why companies would not do that. That, really, was the genesis of this work from which we actually learned something, which is that common sense is extremely uncommon. "The things that everybody knows" doesn't mean that they're being implemented, that they're being done, or that they're being done very effectively.

If you want to bridge the gap between knowing and doing, you have to do two things. First, you have to understand the sources of this gap, whether the gap comes from an absence of courage or from measurement systems that measure the wrong things; whether the gap comes from an emphasis on planning, analysis, and talking rather than doing; or whether the gap comes from the fact that people are so afraid in your organization that they're afraid to do what they know is the right thing, because they're afraid of getting fired, or afraid for their job or all kinds of other things. So the first thing that you need to understand is what the sources of the problem are, and then you need to address the sources.

If the source happens to be fear, you need to do what [Dr. W. Edwards] Deming, the quality guru, used to talk about, which is to drive out fear. If the problem is that people are too engaged in talking and plan-ning rather than doing, you need to em-phasize the organizational equivalent of rapid prototyping, which is very common in the product design world. If the problem is something in your measurement system that is causing people to focus on the wrong things, you need to fix those measures. The solution depends very much, obviously, on the diagnosis of what the problem is.

TAKEAWAYS

- ⚔ Often, companies that want to create high-performance practices and high-performance cultures already have the wisdom needed to deliver changes.

- ⚔ Most companies, however, fail to apply their knowledge, a phenomenon known as the knowing-doing gap.

- ⚔ To bridge the gap between knowing and doing, you must first identify the source or sources of the gap.

- ⚔ After the problem has been identified, you can then address it and implement the appropriate solutions.

Setting Clear and Achievable Goals

Roger Parry

Former Chairman and CEO,
Clear Channel International

SETTING GOALS FROM the perspective of a chief executive really is another way of asking a question about strategy, because the people reporting to a chief executive need to know what's expected of them.

The important thing is to have a really thorough understanding of the issues facing a business, the environment within which it's operating—and, as a result of having an understanding of that environment, you can then set meaningful goals for the management.

Let me give you an example. If you have—as I do at the moment—a business that operates in more than fifty countries, it doesn't necessarily follow that each general manager has exactly the same goal. For our business in China, for example, there is an enormous opportunity to grow. So the goal for the guy running the Chinese business unit is to look for new investments and ways of putting money to work.

If you take the other end of the extreme—which in my case would be Switzerland, where the market is completely mature and satisfied—the goal there for the general manager is about operating efficiency. He is looking to do the same amount of business in a more effective way, whereas his Chinese counterpart is simply looking to do more business.

The lesson is that setting clear goals comes from a really thorough understanding of the business environment in which you are operating.

Another important consideration—and it's a word that I don't think appears in English—is "do-ability." By this I mean, is a goal actually achievable? One of the worst things you can do is to say to an operating manager, "Here is your goal." And the operating manager then looks at you and says, "Such a thing is impossible."

We are all familiar with that in our daily lives. If you say to a child, "I want you to jump over a ten-meter hurdle," the child obviously knows he can't do it and will be very upset. In the same way, if you set—as people do sometimes—business goals that are wholly unachievable, it may make the chief executives feel very macho and tough that they've set people an enormous stretch target, but if the target is unachievable, the only result is going to be very disappointed managers and a general feeling of failure.

Some years ago I was working in an advertising agency group and was responsible for one of the public relations businesses we'd recently acquired. The chief executive told us that he wanted this business to double its sales within two years. Now the problem with doubling your sales within two years in a business like that is that you have to go and hire people to do the work. The constraint actually wasn't winning new clients; the constraint was hiring people, because at the time there was a great shortage.

We went away from that annual budget review knowing in advance that we were going to fail, because it wasn't going to be possible to hire that number of people sufficiently quickly. But the same goal had been set for all the businesses across the whole group, so we were stuck with something we couldn't possibly achieve.

If what went wrong was the original process of setting the goal, everyone has to admit to that and be realistic about it. If you don't have that sort of postmortem, the problem you'll face is that you'll get so many disaffected members of your staff that your whole organization becomes dysfunctional. There will be a lot of people working, feeling this sense of failure. It is very important that people feel a sense of success.

That does not mean that you always set goals that are so easy that everyone achieves them. It's not like an examination process where everybody passes. The important thing is that where a goal is missed, it's missed for reasons that everyone understands, and you can genuinely say, "That was force majeure; that was an external unexpected event." It shouldn't be missed because the original goal was so unrealistic that it couldn't be done.

Clear goals for a business manager come as a result of really understanding the environment within which they're operating, and also as a result of a dialogue between that business manager and his or her chief executive. The right goals are those that both parties understand and buy into, rather than something that just sounds like a very good number to talk about to shareholders.

TAKEAWAYS

- Setting clear and achievable goals really is another way of asking a question about strategy.

- To set meaningful goals, you must thoroughly understand the issues facing the business and the environment within which it's operating.

- You must also set goals that are achievable. Otherwise, the results will be general feelings of disappointment and failure.

- The right goals are those that managers and employees understand and buy into and that are appropriate for the environment in which the business operates.

Managing Projects

John Stewart

Former Director, McKinsey & Company

I THINK ABOUT THE PROBLEMS that
managers get into because they run into
something unfamiliar, and they try to treat
it with familiar approaches. The one that I
see frequently is not understanding when a
problem is really a one-time and unusual
problem versus something that looks like
normal, ongoing activity.

Executing for Results

Having people think about a project as a project is quite useful. Many of us have the same experience when we renovate a house. You always think, "Maybe I can be my own general contractor. I'll deal with the electrician, plumber, plasterer, and mason." And you overrun 20 percent on time and 40 percent on cost. Because one of the things that a contractor does is organize the effort as a project, which most of us don't know how to do. We do it thinking we know how to do it the way we do everything else.

I can remember one auto manufacturing vice president in the States saying, "I will not have a project manager in my business. I have an engineer, a manufacturing person, a marketing person, and a finance person. But I am not going to confuse the organization with a project manager." Well, one auto designed to be 20 percent less expensive than its predecessor ended up being 10 percent more expensive. And late. The project cost, instead of being two billion [dollars], was three billion because of his belief that he could run the business in a normal way in what was really a project.

It's not always clear when one needs a project. You always get the question, "Should I have a project manager when I pick up a pencil or sharpen a pencil?" Well no, not quite. It's when the number of activities that have to be done is greater than one can carry in one's head all the time. Once you get above one hundred different activities and different locations with interdependencies that are not clear, it really is worth the effort.

A project team generally ought to cost somewhere in the neighborhood of 1 percent to 2 percent of the project to have a special group working on the problem. Now, if you have a hundred-million-dollar project and you normally overrun 20 or 30 percent, that's twenty or thirty million dollars. So the choice is, spend an extra million to have a project team and save the twenty- or thirty-million-dollar overrun, which you know is going to happen.

Executing for Results

It seems to me that any middle-management person seeing his organization doing something that is bigger, more complicated, or new ought to think about the power of a separate project organization.

TAKEAWAYS

- Managers can quickly run into trouble when they try to treat unfamiliar problems by using familiar approaches.

- Instead, think about the project as a project, and consider assigning a project manager and team.

- By spending 1 to 2 percent of the project's cost on project management, you can actually save money by preventing overruns and missed deadlines.

Implement Change Quickly When Taking On a New Role

Sir George Cox

Former Director General,
Institute of Directors

THE IMPORTANCE OF MAKING an impact soon after you've taken over a role was brought home to me by a director I worked for when I was a young man running a manufacturing factory. The man took over, he had had a very short overlap with his predecessor, and we sat down at the first Monday morning management meeting with him in the seat. He announced, "We're going to have a lot of change here; it is needed urgently."

I must admit that surprised us as the management team; we didn't think change was that urgent. Sure, things could be improved, but we had thought it was going quite well. He said, "One of the things we're going to do immediately is to cut the number of meetings we have, because we have far too many."

I suppose we agreed, but what we didn't expect was what he said next, which was, "As of today, there are no meetings other than my Monday morning management meeting; and a meeting is more than three people sitting in an office at one time."

We thought, "Wow, that's pretty dramatic."

I said to him, "I'm sure that's an interesting move. Of course, it doesn't include the weekly production meeting I run, with all the foremen, charge-hands, and production chasers?"

"It includes everything," he said.

I started to splutter. "I can't . . ."

And he said, "It's . . . everything."

Bang! All meetings stopped. And a few weeks later I went to him in desperation and said, "I can't run production unless at least once a week I can get together the people who run the various sections of the factory."

"All right," he said. "How long does this meeting last?"

I answered, "It normally starts at 8:00 a.m. and goes through to about 11:00 a.m."

"No," he said, "It starts at 8:00 a.m. and finishes at 9:30 a.m."

"Well, I'll try," I said.

"No, you won't try," he replied. "I'll be there at 9:30 a.m., and if it's still going, I'll break it up."

He asked, "Who do you have at this meeting?"

I replied, "I have my production staff, and I have every charge-hand and every foreman."

He said, "No. You can have either the charge-hand or the foreman."

And that was it.

So that was the meeting I reintroduced. It was half the length of time, and it had half the number of people there—and it worked.

I spoke to this factory director a few years later when I was leaving, and we discussed what happened on this occasion. He said, "We could have tackled the problem of too many meetings by my asking for a list of meetings to review. We'd have shaved little bits off there. What we did was to cut the lot out, and I knew that any that were important enough, we would reintroduce them but on a different basis."

He said, "It was one of the changes I made immediately because you're sitting there and you don't know what to expect. If I'd have been reasonable and looked at how things were going and started to make changes in several months' time, you'd have resisted them. I'd also be much more accepting of the way things were done. So we did a number of things immediately. We changed lots of things and shocked you, but thereafter you knew you were going to get change."

Executing for Results

He explained, "When you take over a role, you come into a very fluid situation. Everyone's looking at what the new boss is going to be like; they don't know what to expect. You have the power then to change almost anything. If you don't do so, it all starts to solidify again. And after that, it's much more difficult to change things."

Whenever I've gone into a role, I've sometimes seen immediately the things that need changing. At other times you're not too sure what those big changes should be. And you don't want to do anything precipitant that might damage the business, so you change some of the smaller things. It might be a physical change. But you make a number of changes that get across to people that things are going to be different.

Scrapping meetings wasn't the biggest thing this factory director did, but it sent a signal: "I'm going to manage things differently; we're going to operate to different and much tighter standards." It wasn't a strategic decision, but it showed that things were different.

Executing for Results

So anywhere I've been, I've always tried to make a point quite quickly by changing something—often quite small, almost cosmetic—to make it clear that things are going to be different.

In business today, you have change all the time. Getting a business that responds to change and is flexible, and where people think flexibly, is very important. You're always pushing every area to get better at something. When you take over a situation, you need to get across immediately that things are going to change for the better. You're interested in hearing what people have to say, but lots of things are going to change and be done differently immediately, because that sets a pattern.

TAKEAWAYS

- When you're a manager taking over a new role, it's critical to quickly implement changes to symbolize that things are going to be different.

- During the transition period, the situation is fluid. Employees don't know what to expect, and they will look to you to set the tone.

- These changes can be small, and even nonstrategic, but they are needed to prepare teams for a more flexible future.

- Implementing change quickly sets the pattern for a new direction and helps employees realize immediate changes for the better.

Don't Over-Detail

Colin Day

Group Chief Financial Officer, Reckitt Benckiser

ONE OF THE EARLY THINGS I learned
in business was when you do and don't need
detail. When I was somewhat more junior in
finance, in the electronics company where I
was a controller, we prided ourselves on having a lot of reports and an excessive amount
of reporting. At the time it seemed very
valuable.

Executing for Results

I recall working inordinately long hours producing this stuff. Now, as I look back, the reason for it all is beyond me. One of the key lessons I learned is that detail won't save a company if it gets into trouble because you have the wrong product strategy or the wrong marketing mix.

We produced statistics, numbers, and analysis for people, and, quite frankly, it was not possible to read. Nobody could read this stuff and digest it. We were so immersed in the detail that it was a key reason why, when the market went one way, the business went the other.

It was only afterward when I looked back that I thought to myself, "This is not the way to go forward. This is not the way to run a business." For me, one of the key lessons that I've tried to implement with my people going forward in subsequent businesses is, don't over-detail. Keep it very simple and manage your business with some key performance indicators (KPIs).

A recent example came when we had a presentation from one of our subsidiaries.

They had produced two hundred or more charts to justify doing a relatively simple business reorganization. They had allowed themselves nearly an hour for this thing, and when it came to it, it was a case of, "What do you want?"

"We want to do X-Y-Z."

"Okay. Do you have three or four key charts?"

"Yes."

"Fine, show us those."

Boom.

"Agreed. Next?"

These guys stood up on the platform with the other one hundred ninety-six charts, not sure if we were serious or whether we were firing them or not taking them seriously.

The fact is, you don't need two hundred charts to make the point. Over the years, since those early days in the electronics business, I've worked hard to spread that message.

Too many people hide behind detail for justification or confidence purposes rather than using years of training and management experience to build a decision based more on intuition than on figures. There's not enough of that. You need more gut feel and instinct than mass data.

The critical elements in the detail that you concentrate on will be, what's it doing to my top line, sales and revenues? Is it grabbing my market share? Am I gaining against the competition? What's the return on investment? Does it add to the bottom line? That's about four or five pages, and two or three charts. It's about a key recommendation. If you can't do it in four or five minutes, there's something wrong.

TAKEAWAYS

⚎ Companies frequently compile enormous amounts of data, reports, and analyses that most people, in the end, can't even understand.

Executing for Results

⚌ To maintain focus on the business and
its markets, don't "over-detail."

⚌ Further, avoid hiding behind detail to
justify your actions. Rely instead on
your experience and intuition for
guidance.

⚌ Concentrate on the critical elements
in any recommendation. If you need
two hundred charts to make a point,
you're missing the point.

Reduce Complexity, Don't Analyze It

Stuart Grief

*Vice President, Strategy and Business
Development, Textron*

ON NEGOTIATING COMPLEX, large,
high-risk situations, I would say that there
are an awful lot of experts on negotiation
out there. I'm not going to claim to be one

of them. I would say that I have observed a pretty common behavior in these situations. And part of it was driven by the fact that there is so much information available today to anybody doing analysis on a business issue, far more than there has ever been before.

The thing that I've observed that is common across all these situations is that they get much more complex than they need to be. In more than twenty years plus of doing business analysis, I don't think I've seen a spreadsheet from others—or, I'm as guilty as they are and that I've created myself—that doesn't have two or three times more complexity than it needs to have.

As an example, I was working with a client once on expanding into China in the automotive sector. One of the analyses that was necessary for this very complex decision process—and negotiation for the investment budget to move into China—was really what the fleet of cars in China was going to look like downstream. This is going back ten years ago, when there was a lot of uncertainty about how China was likely to evolve.

But the spreadsheet that was developed, or the model that was developed, had so much information in it. In addition to population and wealth, which were really the key drivers of automobile consumption, there were tons of factors related to geo-political stability, the distribution of population across the country, and so on. There were just so many factors that were built into it. They were all very interesting factors but, at the end of the day, they would move the needle by 5 percent or 10 percent, when the crystal ball was already far more imprecise than that was.

The problem that that raised was that in the course of a four-hour debate and dia-logue on what the appropriate investment should be, three-quarters of that time was spent debating these less-important issues because they were put out there. All of this data ends up being like raw meat for people to debate in these sessions, as opposed to getting focused on what the heart of the matter really is and agreeing on what the heart of the matter is, which is equally important, and then focusing the dialogue on those points.

So rather than debating whether or not the population is likely to move west in China, there should have been a debate around [the fact that] given that the number of cars is likely to be about 6.1 and 6.3 million, what the demand is going to look like and what can be done to go after it.

That is, ultimately, what I think is most helpful in complex situations, whether it's an internal decision-making process or negotiations with an outsider. Scope the discussion around the things that truly matter, and get everything else off the table so that people can stay focused.

Somebody once said to me—and I thought it was a very good way of capturing this lesson—that in any complex situation, the effort should be on reducing complexity rather than analyzing complexity. If you do

that, it seems that, in my experience, we'll
be able to take a lot more ground more
quickly than otherwise.

TAKEAWAYS

- More information is available today to
  those doing business analysis than ever
  before.

- The result is that business discussions
  and supporting reports become more
  complex than necessary, often by as
  much as two or three times.

- When this happens, key discussions
  switch focus from what really matters
  to debates about less-important
  issues.

Executing for Results

꤄ In any complex situation, focus your efforts on reducing complexity rather than analyzing it. By doing so you'll move forward more quickly.

Seek Simplicity and You'll Get It

Sir Gerry Robinson

Former Non-Executive Chairman,
Allied Domecq

I'M A GREAT BELIEVER in keeping things simple. The natural tendency among people who run something is to complicate it—to pretend that somehow it is more complicated than it is. And it's very unhelpful, because most things are simple. Often people are complicated; sometimes the product is complicated. But the business itself rarely is; it's about very simple things.

I remember once when I went along with the strategy director of Lex Service Group, and we were trying to buy a lighting company that hired out lighting to the film business. It was owned by two guys in East London. The guy I went with was asking incredibly complicated questions. The basic question was, "How do you arrive at pricing?" And he was asking, "Is it strategically related to the price of the product? Is it to do with the capital cost? Is it to do with the average let period?"

I was very junior at the time, and I could see these two guys looking at one another in confusion. One replied, "No, no. What happens is that David writes the price he thinks it should be on a piece of paper, and I write it on a piece of paper. Then we choose the higher of the two."

This business was absolutely flourishing. And I thought, "God, how obvious is that? You try it out. It's a small business. Don't go into massive calculations about how you price. Test something out in a very simple way. If it works, do it." There's just such clarity about that—it was just so clear and obvious.

I think that happens a lot. We go into all sorts of machinations about quite simple things when, actually, we can just try it. The way you avoid complicating things in an organization is always to ask, "What does that mean? Why are you saying it like that? Do you mean this? Or do you mean that?"

Whenever something comes at you that is gobbledygook, that's the first sign of complication. Say, "I don't understand; tell me again." And then if it's something simple—which it nearly always is—ask, "Why don't you just say that? Why don't you just do that?" It comes from you. Be willing to genuinely say when you don't understand something, because very often people won't do that. Be prepared to do that, and then say, "Hang on, does that mean that? Why didn't you say that? Why didn't you deal with it like that?"

Executing for Results

If you seek simplicity, you'll get it; and you will encourage it in others.

TAKEAWAYS

- ≼ There is a natural tendency among people who run something to complicate it, to pretend it is more complicated than it is.

- ≼ Often, however, most things are simple. It's the people who complicate it.

- ≼ Rather than get into massive calculations and "gobbledygook" when trying new ideas, just do a simple test.

- ≼ Also, be willing to admit when you don't understand something. Seek simplicity, and you'll get it.

You Need Clarity and Commitment to Execute

Liam McGee

*President, Global Consumer and Small
Business Bank, Bank of America Corporation*

ONE OF THE HALLMARKS of our com-
pany, in my view, is our ability to execute.
And most third-party observers would say
that about us. Some might not even view

that as an attribute, but they would say it is a hallmark of our company. We do get things done.

I think [there are] a couple of components there. We're willing to make a decision. We gather facts, we get together—either a few people, or ultimately it may be me. Be decisive; make a decision; create clarity. And then, in general, run through fire; don't walk through it.

Sometimes the decisions you have to make and execute are challenging. They're difficult. They may impact individuals, communities, and customers. But our general philosophy—and my general philosophy—is, be decisive; make the decision; and then run through the fire. It's better for everybody, that certainty, that clarity.

There are some companies, some managers, who struggle to make a clear decision; there's waffling and ambiguity. Then they want to please everybody, so they walk very slowly, and that doesn't please anybody because most people want to know where you're going and want to get it done and get to the other side.

Executing for Results

In our company, the best examples of our ability and willingness to execute would be when we put companies together. We believe that somebody has to be in charge. You can't have co-heads; you can't have co-CEOs. There needs to be somebody in charge; define that up front. Define the process to make decisions, make the decisions, and then move on.

We have evolved pretty dramatically as a company. I think that the Fleet Bank combination and MBNA—now U.S. Trust—are examples of us doing that. We do put someone in charge—maybe from the acquired company, maybe from our company—but there's clarity of who's in charge. There's clarity of the process to make decisions. [Decisions are] fact-based—not political, not based on who won or who lost.

A great example of that is when we bought MBNA. The old model would have been to just take the Bank of America processes and hoist them on there. That was a decision that I was not comfortable making, because we had an opportunity here by putting these two companies together to create something that was much better than either one of them could have been separately or even just by slamming them together.

We picked a lot of the MBNA systems, processes, and leaders, because we thought it gave us a much better chance to have a transformational or transcendent card business, which is going to be necessary as that business is getting tougher. But it didn't preclude our ability and willingness to make that decision.

We made that decision early on, and we communicated it. Some of the Bank of America teammates weren't happy with that, but it was certainty, it was clarity, and it gave us a road map to move on and run through the fire, if you will.

TAKEAWAYS

⚔ The ability to execute successfully re-
quires a willingness to make a decision.
Gather the facts, get together, and see
the decision through.

⚔ Some of your decisions may be challenging to make and execute, and they
may have an impact on individuals,
communities, and customers.

⚔ Realize that you can't please everyone.
Always make a clear decision, and
communicate that decision clearly.

⚔ After a decision has been made, espe-
cially one that is unpopular, commit
to that decision and implement it
quickly.

Standardize Practices Across Business Functions

Robert Herbold

Former Chief Operating Officer,
Microsoft Corporation

ONE OF THE THINGS that I ran into when I joined Microsoft in 1994, after twenty-six years at Procter & Gamble, was a real organizational mess. The reason I was hired at Microsoft was to take the business issues off of Bill Gates's desk, because he didn't enjoy doing those things. He wanted time against the products. Steve Ballmer was running sales, and I had the other things.

At the end of the quarter, the first quarter that I was there, after two or three weeks, we still didn't have the numbers because the finance people were massaging all this data that they were getting from all these subsidiaries and divisions. And I couldn't understand it. I went over to the finance organization, and they showed me just what a zoo they had on their hands, because all the subsidiaries had become very independent.

The German subsidiary had developed its own charter of accounts and hired a bunch of people to develop some new information systems. They realized their marketing budget was a little high, and so they took parts of marketing, redefined them, and put them up in cost of goods sold. They were not being unethical; they were just being advocates for their work.

Executing for Results

But then you go to Italy, and they're doing something different. And you go to the U.S., and they're handling it another way. At the end of the quarter, that all comes together, and you realize what a mess you have. We had to clean this up.

Also, the staffing was out of control. At that German subsidiary, they had more than seventy IT people, and this was supposed to be a sales subsidiary. They had seventy IT people, and they built their own data center. People just get out of control when they're fairly successful, and the business was growing 30 to 40 percent a year at this stage. So they had a lot of revenue to cover up a multitude of sins, and that's really what was occurring. It was clear.

Bill Gates came into my office about three and a half weeks after the close of the quarter and said, "What are the numbers?"

And I said, "You son of gun, you created this mess; you know why I don't have the numbers."

So what did we do? We took—I took—one individual from finance who I knew had been there six or seven years and was highly experienced; he was in the controller area. And I took an IT person who was familiar with the existing systems who had been with the company seven or eight years. I said to these two individuals, "You're going to be the leaders of this team. The finance person is in charge; the IT person will work very closely with him; and you will form a small team. First of all, in the next couple of weeks, we want you to define the chart of accounts that will be used throughout the company, and we also want you to define the architecture of the systems that you're going to develop in order to clean up this mess."

In eleven months they rolled this thing out, and we literally were able to move out of the IT organization hundreds and hundreds of people. This was in a company that was growing 30 to 40 percent. They were able to eliminate hundreds of information systems, so in that German subsidiary that had seventy-two IT people, we cut it down to two. We eliminated their data center and told them their job was to sell. Their job was not to be creative in regard to the general ledger and build fancy new information systems. What we wanted to do was the basics, and we wanted to be able to close the books in forty-eight hours.

Well, we had all the data on one database in Redmond, Washington. You could get to it from these Web-based menus from anywhere in the world. I could be in a hotel in Hong Kong, an office in Germany, or in my office in Redmond. I'd name the time period, the products, and, boom, there's the key information I needed. It was a thing of beauty.

After we finished this project, it then became the showcase for presenting to customers how they should manage their company using Microsoft software. It turned out to be an incredible sales tool while also solving this mess at Microsoft. And it was a powerful experience to go through to understand the power of simplicity and the power of clear delegation of very specific criteria as to what you want to happen.

Executing for Results

What did I learn from that experience? What I learned was that in these functional areas like IT, HR, finance, or manufacturing, if you let that fragment and let all the subsidiaries and divisions go off and do their own thing and then have a central group that attempts to pull this stuff together with some sanity, you are in for heavy weather. You need some crisp, standardized measures to know what's happening in the organization.

TAKEAWAYS

- ⚑ When the various subsidiaries and divisions of an organization are charged with reporting their own numbers, an organizational mess is inevitable.

- ⚑ Instead of having a central group that tries to compile and interpret the various numbers, develop standardized measures that can be implemented across the organization.

⚔ When you create such a plan, delegate clearly and use very specific criteria for defining what you want to happen.

⚔ Doing so helps you to understand not only what's happening in any given business unit but also what's happening throughout the organization.

Concentrating on the Core Aspects of Your Business

Sir Nick Scheele

*Former President and Chief
Operating Officer,
Ford Motor Company*

Executing for Results

WHEN I WENT BACK to North America in August 2001 and took over running North America and ultimately, later that year, [became] President of the company, it was clear that we were in some difficulty. We were losing money, we had had some very poor launches, and there was a lot of confusion. We'd been distracted in large measure by diversionary activities, by buying up companies, by moving into other areas. It was very clear we needed to get back to our business.

In my first meeting—which was videoed around North America—with the company management and a lot of people working in North America, I coined a phrase, which was "Back to Basics." And basics in our business—the car business, the automotive business—was really four things. What do we do? What are the basics of our job?

This is what I said, "[The basics] are designing, engineering, manufacturing, and wholesaling great cars and trucks. That's what we exist to do, and that's what we should be doing. Our jobs should all be related to that. If anything doesn't add up in those four things (designing, engineering, wholesaling, and manufacturing), and then if you add the credit company, financing—if it doesn't support one of those five elements, you should be saying, 'What am I doing this for? What is my role in this? How am I supporting the basics of our business?'"

I think everyone should look at that and say, "I'll stack my job up against those five things, and if I'm not doing 100 percent of my work in support of that, I probably need to question it."

That Back to Basics is something that I think is fundamental. We should be doing it all the time because things change. The external environment changes; fads and fancies change; and we add things. And they tend to be distractions. We should always go back and say, "Is it Back to Basics?"

As we do that, we should keep it simple, because most businesses are pretty simple. It's the execution that delivers the ultimate result. We need to have people focused simply on what they can do to support the objectives of the company, corporation, business, or enterprise. If they're not focused on it, they're probably really not contributing to the maximum ability that they offer the organization.

If we look at things in that way, we will have a much more self-fulfilling business proposition, which will deliver a better bottom line. And out of that lesson of Back to Basics, which is still the mantra of the company around the globe—Back to Basics: design, engineer, manufacture, wholesale, and finance—everybody looks at it in that light today. That is also a change because you rarely have a mantra that lasts for five years or more. Now, it's lasting five years and more.

What I learned out of the Back to Basics and Keep It Simple was that everyone needs to know how their job contributes to the goals and the objectives of the corporation. And when they do know it, they can really focus on giving it 100 percent of their energy and delivering the results that are so necessary.

The other lesson I sadly had to learn was: don't be beguiled by management gurus, fads of the month, flavors of this, and how to diversify to get yourself better. Concentrate; remain focused on your business. If you do that, you will have a better business as a result.

TAKEAWAYS

- 🏷 When a company is losing money and is in a general state of confusion, it is time to get "Back to Basics."

- 🏷 Getting back to basics means that everyone in the organization should be working in support of the core aspects of the business.

Executing for Results

🔁 Then, when working toward these core elements, it's important to "Keep It Simple." Execution delivers the final results.

🔁 When people know how their jobs contribute to the organization's goals and give 100 percent focus and energy, they will deliver a better bottom line.

Never Forget the Importance of Details

J. W. Marriott, Jr.

Chairman and CEO,
Marriott International

I WAS BROUGHT UP by a great mentor in our company. He was my father, and he was a stickler for details. He was a perfectionist, which made him very difficult to work for because nothing was ever perfect. And I was certainly not even close to being perfect. I was consistently reminded of that, but I was also reminded by him of the great importance of the details, particularly in the restaurant business, which is what he grew up in, what I grew up in, and which is the foundation of our business.

Back in the late seventies, he found AstroTurf to be an attractive product to put down on the sidewalks that were not colored, on open balconies of hotels that were just in concrete, and around pool decks, which then were concrete. He loved this green look of the AstroTurf. And he was constantly badgering me to get more Astro-Turf down and to refresh our hotels and make them look better by putting around AstroTurf.

This conversation continued for many, many years. Finally—it was 1982, and it was in May—and I remember it very clearly. I was in my office, and they came in and said, "The landowner for the site in New York that you have selected to build the New York Marriott Marquis hotel is on the phone." It was in the Times Square area. It was at that time a very seedy area, a very run-down area. We had been rumored to build this hotel and were making the decision to build it. A lot of the major publications said we were crazy and that we shouldn't do it; it was a high risk. But I was pretty convinced that this was a great place to be. The land-owner said, "Your option to buy the land runs out tonight at midnight; you have to make a decision about what you're going to do."

The head of construction came into my office, and he said, "You're going to have to go along with the contractor. You've asked for a no-strike clause; you can't get one. If you have a strike during construction, you're going to be delayed. It's going to run your costs way up."

And the mayor's office called and said, "We understand you're going to announce that you're going ahead with this hotel. We want to be there for the announcement; we would like to get credit for it."

It was a big decision. I had people running in and out with all kinds of problems, and then my secretary said my dad was on the phone. I picked up the phone, and he said, "When are you going to put the Astro-Turf on the balconies of your new hotel in Washington?"

And I thought, "Here I am, making the biggest decision I've ever been faced with in this business—the biggest amount of money we've ever spent on a hotel, a high-risk hotel in a tough neighborhood—and he wants to know about the AstroTurf on the balconies of the first hotel we really built: Twin Bridges."

I was brought right back down to earth. Yes, okay, I'm making a big deal here. But you better not take your eye off the details; you'd better worry about the details in the business. And I do. I'm always worried about the details. They say I'm into too much detail. But I grew up in the business, and I grew up learning the details, focusing on the details, and worrying about the details. I really don't believe you can make good strategic decisions unless you understand the business and have a feeling for the detail that goes into what makes the business work.

This is a very complex business. The hotel business is far more than just making up a hotel room, cleaning it, and renting it. You have a lot of technology issues in developing the business—huge reservation systems, great advertising and marketing systems, huge maintenance problems with these hotels, capital reinvestment problems, zoning problems, titlement problems. There are all kinds of issues as you develop and build this business. And food and beverage by itself is just a huge business, very different from the hotel business but an integral part of it.

I've had to learn the details and focus on the details, and I've found that learning and focusing on the details has helped me make better strategic decisions. It's been easier for me to make those decisions as I've tried to stay up with what's going on at as many levels of the business as I can.

I get out of the office. I get out of the office to visit the properties. I'll visit two hundred fifty hotels this year. I'll visit another fifty sites that we're looking at to build and develop properties, whether it's time-share or hotels. I see the sites and the properties, and I'm out there kicking the tires, trying to find out what's going on, asking questions, and listening to the general managers and management teams. I'll get the management teams together, and I'll ask, "What are some of your biggest issues? What are we doing to help you? Are you getting the support you need from headquarters? How's business? What's your competition doing?" I've spent a lot of time studying the competition, reading about them, visiting their hotels, and seeing what's new. I'm just out there. I think you have to be out there.

My dad used to say that the swivel chair is the biggest problem in the executive life,

because it's so comfortable, you don't want
to get out of it. But you have to get out of
the swivel chair, get out of the office, and
find out what's going on.

TAKEAWAYS

- ⚔ Even when problems are rampant and
  big deals are at risk, you can't under-
  estimate the importance of paying attention to the details.

- ⚔ Without a firm grasp of the details that
  make the business work, you won't be
  able to make sound strategic decisions.

- ⚔ Take the time to learn and focus on
  the details, stay abreast of as many levels of your business as possible, and ask
  questions.

Executing for Results

❧ Make the effort to get out of your comfortable swivel chair and find out what's going on, not only with your own business but also with your competition.

You Don't Need a Formal Position to Make Things Happen

Rosabeth Moss Kanter

*Professor of Business Administration,
Harvard Business School*

Executing for Results

As I saw the world globalizing, I saw that more things were happening worldwide, where no one country or community could capture all of enterprise. I would take long-distance trips where I'd often feel homesick. I'd come home to Boston and wonder what the impact was on my home community.

Because I was feeling the distance in the world, I wanted to get more involved in my home community and I wondered how to have an impact. I knew that people back home in Boston were not seeing the exciting opportunities emerging around the world.

In the U.S. at that time, there was concern about foreigners taking our jobs. Yet what I saw was hunger for the goods and services and the know-how that came out of my home city, the United States, and the Western world.

I had had a conversation with a very savvy person I knew—having been involved in state politics in Massachusetts—somebody who

had been key in the presidential election. I
kept saying to him, "Why aren't people paying attention? This is such an important
issue."

He had said to me, "Why don't you do
something about it?"

I asked, "What can I do? I'm just a single
individual."

He said, "You have the power of Harvard
behind you. You can convene, forge alliances, and bring people to the table."

And that's what I did.

I created a partnership with two of the
big business associations in Boston—the
Greater Boston Chamber of Commerce
and the main industry Federation of Manu-
facturers—and we did a survey. We asked
questions, and we found out the ties: where
were people getting their raw materials,
their ideas, and their customers? How was
that moving outside of our home region to
other places?

To do that, I had to convince people that
this was an important issue; they didn't

believe it automatically. I had to show them that this was happening in many other places, so I formed partnerships in four other cities in the United States, where I had connections or knew somebody who could be a local partner, and started opening up that local community.

The data we collected put facts and figures behind the issue; I convened people and encouraged local people around the country to convene people. I went and spoke in all of those cities. It was invented out of a sense that there was something that needed to be done. It had a very big impact. It led to my book *World Class*, about how you could thrive locally, even in the global economy. I was invited to all kinds of gatherings where I could influence the thinking of mayors and regional public officials all over the world.

For me, the personal lessons were that I didn't have to wait for somebody to appoint me to a board or a commission. I had become accustomed, as a well-known person, to having people invite me. I didn't have to create opportunities; they'd come to me. But here, in order to establish an idea that people were not yet talking or thinking about, I had to take the initiative.

I saw how easy it was to have an idea, go to established organizations, and say, "I will help you. I will do some of the work and give you an opportunity to bring something new to your members. We can bring people together and make a big splash that'll be good for you." It was possible to move an idea forward. I learned about creating complex coalitions and alliances.

Even inside a company, you can use the same principles. When I speak, the most frequently asked question from middle managers is, "What do you do—if you're not the CEO—to change the company?" I say that there are three things you can do.

The first is demonstration. You can take your own area of the company and demonstrate everything that you think the rest of the company should be doing in a microcosm, in your own department. But the other two things are very much like my story of *World Class*: education and collaboration.

Collaboration first: you can always find allies and peers in the company. Bring them to the table, and talk about their issues and agendas and how you can advance a common agenda going forward. In education: anybody can gather data, do a survey, find the facts, convene a lunch, and bring people to the table.

The power of convening and the power of voice—naming problems, speaking them out loud, bringing data and facts to bear on the situation, and doing it with allies, colleagues, and other departments—is exactly the same principle, applied inside the company, that I used in my complex regional coalitions in Boston, Miami, Seattle, South Carolina, and Cleveland.

TAKEAWAYS

- ⚔ To bring important global ideas back home and effect change, you needn't be an executive. You just need to be willing to take the initiative.

- ⚔ Start by collecting facts and figures, and then begin convincing people in your own department that the issue is important.

- ⚔ Next, find allies and peers outside your department to develop a plan to advance a common agenda, and then educate others about your cause.

- ⚔ You can use the power of convening and the power of voice to make both big and small changes; you just have to be willing to try.

Execution

Domenico De Sole

Former President and CEO, Gucci Group

IN 1994 I WAS STILL managing Gucci America, but the whole group suffered dramatically because the last family member running the company clearly was not up to the task. So when the company almost collapsed in 1993, the then shareholder, a company called Investcorp, asked me to move to Italy and see if I could fix the company.

Tom Ford, the creative director, and I took control of the company. We agreed that we needed to pursue the same general strategy that had been outlined by the prior CEO; in fact I'd worked with the prior CEO in outlining that strategy. The strategy sounded good, but every time something was done, there seemed to be a problem or it was poorly done. We had a company really going bankrupt because of failure to properly execute what we thought was a good strategy.

What we did differently, which made a dramatic change for the better, was just simple execution. We understood what needed to be done, and, most importantly, we did it well. Attention to detail and everything that needed to be done in terms of developing a collection, selling a collection—every single detail—was worked on: production, delivery of product, quality of service in the store, refurbishment in the store. Everything suddenly started to be executed well.

Make sure that everything is done with accuracy and on budget if it is an issue with money. Make sure everybody understands who's doing what and when. Really have a complete understanding of how the company operates, and intervene at the appropriate time.

[When it comes to] managing situations, sometimes I really see that what happens in companies is that people don't talk to each other. They like to talk to the boss because people report to one boss, but they don't talk to each other.

We had a lot of problems with the prior CEO, who was viewed as inconsistent. There was no consistency between what he was preaching and what he was doing. It's very important to lead by example. I am a workaholic in a way. I always work very hard, but I worked particularly hard back in 1994, because I felt it was my duty to show everybody that I was not asking them to do anything that I wouldn't do myself anyway. At that point the company was much smaller, so it was easier for me. I was the chief operating officer of the company, CEO, head of merchandising; basically I was doing a lot.

So within a smaller company, Tom and I did a very effective job of spreading the gospel and the mission about the company.

It is impossible to succeed with everything immediately, so you really have to understand what's tactical or what's strategic to have a sense of what you are doing. Is that the wrong strategy? Or is it the right strategy and you don't have the right people? Or is the execution not good? It's really important in business to have a good understanding of why things work or why things don't work, and sometimes to be realistic about the amount of time that it takes to get things done.

As my experience at Gucci has taught me, excellent execution is everything.

TAKEAWAYS

⚔ To improve results, focus on simple execution. Find out what needs to be done, and then do it well.

⚔ To execute effectively, be accurate and on budget. Be sure that everyone understands who's doing what and when, and ensure that they know how the company operates.

⚔ It's also important to lead by example. Be consistent both in what you're preaching and in what you're doing.

⚔ Realize that change may not be immediate. In such cases, be realistic about what's needed to get things done and the time it will require.

⚔ ABOUT THE ⚔
CONTRIBUTORS

Sir George Cox is the former Director General of Institute of Directors. He is currently Chairman of the United Kingdom's Design Council.

Sir George started out as an aeronautical engineer and factory manager. He formed the IT consulting and research company Butler Cox in 1977. He developed the company and floated it on the London Stock Exchange, before presiding over its sale to Computer Sciences in 1991.

He was Managing Director, and then Chairman, of Unisys U.K. Additionally, as Senior Independent Director of the London International Financial Futures and Options Exchange (LIFFE) until 2002, he played a significant part in overseeing the restructuring and turnaround of the Exchange.

In 1999 he became Director General of the Institute of Directors (IoD), an organization that represents individual company directors in the United Kingdom. During his tenure he launched new premises in seven other cities, introduced plans for the IoD's first overseas site in Paris, and introduced a "Chartered Director" program offering accredited assessment of board-level competence. He left in 2004 when he joined Design Council.

About the Contributors

Sir George is Director of the U.K. bank Bradford & Bingley Plc., Director of Shorts (a division of Bombardier Aerospace), and a member of the supervisory board of NYSE Euronext, Inc. He is also a member of the council of Warwick University and sits on the advisory board of Warwick Business School.

Colin Day is Chief Financial Officer and Director of Reckitt Benckiser, a leading provider of cleaning and health and personal products.

Mr. Day started his career in 1973 as a trainee accountant at Eastman Kodak Company. A year later he joined British Gas, where he worked as an internal audit, management, and project accountant for five years.

In 1980 he moved to De La Rue Group, the world's largest commercial security printer, where he spent eight years in various financial and accounting roles within the group and its Crosfield Electronics subsidiary. By the end of his tenure, he had risen to Group Financial Controller.

In 1988 he joined the power and automation technology company ABB Group as Group Finance Director of ABB Kent, Plc., moving up to become Group Finance Director of ABB Instrumentation Ltd. In 1995 he became Group Finance Director at marketing communications company Aegis Group, Plc., a position he held until 2000.

Mr. Day has been Group Chief Financial Officer and Director of Reckitt Benckiser since 2005.

He has also held positions as Director of easyJet Airline Company, Ltd. and Bell Group, Plc. He became Director of WPP Group, Plc. in 2005.

Domenico De Sole is the former President and CEO of Gucci Group NV, a leading multibrand luxury goods company.

Mr. De Sole moved from Italy to the United States in 1970, where he earned a master's degree from Harvard University and became a partner in the Washington law firm of Patton, Boggs & Blow. He joined Gucci in 1984 as CEO of Gucci America. He remained in New York until 1994, when he moved to Italy as Gucci Group's Chief Operating Officer.

He was appointed CEO, and at the end of 1995 led Gucci Group's listing on the New York and Amsterdam stock exchanges. In 1999 he successfully fought a hostile takeover bid, securing Gucci's independence as a basis for continued expansion, which has included the acquisition of Yves Saint Laurent, Alexander McQueen, and Stella McCartney.

Mr. De Sole left Gucci in 2004. The same year he joined the board of Gap, Inc. He is also a director of Bausch & Lomb, Inc.; Telecom Italia, S.p.A, and Delta Air Lines, Inc.

Stuart Grief is the Vice President of Strategy and Business Development at Textron, one of the world's largest and most successful multi-industry companies.

About the Contributors

Prior to joining Textron, Mr. Grief served as Vice President and Director at Boston Consulting Group (BCG). During his fourteen-year tenure, he was a senior member of the U.S. Industrial Goods and Automotive practices and a leader of the Corporate Finance and Strategy practice. His expertise in the areas of business development, market and portfolio strategy, and operations includes client work in market segmentation, growth strategies, and restructuring and business integration. He also led BCG's recruiting activities in Boston for five years.

In July 2004, Mr. Grief joined Textron. As Vice President of Strategy and Business Development, he works closely with senior leadership across the enterprise to create and implement business unit and corporate strategies that drive growth, profitability, and shareholder value creation. In addition, Mr. Grief is a corporate officer and a member of the Transformation Leadership Team.

Robert Herbold is the former Chief Operating Officer and Executive Vice President of Microsoft Corporation. He is currently the Managing Director of the consulting business The Herbold Group, LLC.

Mr. Herbold joined Microsoft in 1994 as Chief Operating Officer and Executive Vice President. For the following six and a half years, he was responsible for finance, manufacturing and distribution, information systems, human resources, corporate marketing, market research, and public relations. During his tenure as COO, Microsoft experienced a fourfold increase in revenue and a sevenfold increase in profits.

From spring 2001 until June 2003, Mr. Herbold worked part-time for Microsoft as Executive Vice President, assisting in the government, industry, and customer areas.

Prior to his time at Microsoft, Mr. Herbold spent twenty-six years at Procter & Gamble. During his last five years with P&G, he was Senior Vice President of Advertising and Information Services, responsible for the company's worldwide advertising and brand management operations, all marketing-related services, and management information systems worldwide.

Mr. Herbold serves as Director of Agilent Technologies, Inc.; ICOS Corporation (a subsidiary of Eli Lilly and Company); and First Mutual Bank. He recently authored the book *The Fiefdom Syndrome.*

Mr. Herbold was appointed by President George W. Bush to the President's Council of Advisors on Science and Technology Policy. He currently chairs the council's Education Subcommittee.

J. W. Marriott, Jr., is Chairman and CEO of Marriott International, Inc., one of the world's largest lodging companies. His leadership spans more than fifty years, and he has taken Marriott from a family restaurant business to a global lodging company with more than twenty-eight hundred properties in sixty-eight countries and territories.

About the Contributors

During high school and college, Mr. Marriott was employed by the Hot Shoppes restaurant chain, where he worked in a variety of positions.

He joined Marriott full-time in 1956 and soon afterward took over management of the company's first hotel. Mr. Marriott became Executive Vice President of the company and then, in 1964, became its President. He was elected CEO in 1972 and Chairman in 1985.

Mr. Marriott serves on the boards of Sunrise Assisted Living and the National Urban League and is Director of the Naval Academy Endowment Trust and the National Geographic Society. He is a member of the U.S. Travel and Tourism Promotional Advisory Board, the World Travel & Tourism Council, and the National Business Council.

He also chairs the President's Export Council and the Leadership Council of the Laura Bush Foundation for America's Libraries.

Liam McGee is President of Global Consumer and Small Business Banking at Bank of America Corporation.

Mr. McGee joined Bank of America in 1990 and has broad leadership experience in consumer and commercial banking, as well as technology and operations. He led the California Consumer Bank, and Corporate Technology and Operations, before he was named President of Bank of America California. In 2001 he was appointed President of the Bank of America Consumer Bank.

About the Contributors

Mr. McGee is a member of the National Urban League Board of Trustees and the Arts & Science Council Board of Directors in Charlotte, North Carolina. He has also served as Chairman of the University of San Diego Board of Trustees and the United Way of Greater Los Angeles, and two terms as Director of the Federal Reserve Bank of San Francisco.

Rosabeth Moss Kanter is a renowned Harvard Business School professor (holding the Ernest L. Arbuckle Chair) and bestselling author whose strategic and practical insights have guided leaders of large and small organizations for more than twenty-five years.

She is the former editor of *Harvard Business Review* (1989–1992) and a consultant to major corporations and governments worldwide on issues of strategy, innovation, and leadership for change. She has been named to lists of the "50 most powerful women in the world" (*Times* of London), placed in the top 10 on the annual list of the "50 most influential business thinkers in the world" (Accenture and Thinkers 50), and called one of the nine "rock stars of business" (American Way).

Professor Kanter is the author or coauthor of seventeen books, with translations into seventeen languages. Her classic prizewinning book *Men and Women of the Corporation* was a source of insight to countless individuals and organizations about corporate careers and the individual and organizational factors that can load the situation for success; a spin-off cartoon video, *A Tale of "O": On Being Different,* is among the world's most widely used diversity tools; and a related book, *Work and Family in the United States,* set a policy agenda (in 2001 a coalition of centers created the Rosabeth Moss Kanter Award for the best research on that issue).

Her award-winning book *When Giants Learn to Dance* showed many companies worldwide the way to master the new terms of competition at the dawn of the global information age. Her latest book is *America the Principled: 6 Opportunities for Becoming a Can-Do Nation Once Again.*

Roger Parry is the former Chairman and CEO of Clear Channel International, the world's leading out-of-home media company operating across radio, outdoor advertising, and live entertainment.

Mr. Parry spent the first seven years of his career as a reporter and producer, working for the BBC and commercial television and radio. He then became a consultant with McKinsey & Company, where he had a range of clients across marketing strategy and post-merger integration.

He moved on to become Development Director of Aegis Group, Plc., a marketing communications company. In this role he was part of the team that managed the successful restructuring and refinancing of Aegis in 1992.

He was CEO of More Group, Inc. from 1995 to 1998, when it was acquired by Clear Channel. Mr.

About the Contributors

Parry was CEO of Clear Channel International for six years. He became Chairman in 2004 and left in 2005.

He is currently Chairman of newspaper publisher Johnston Press, Plc.; Mobile Streams, Plc.; and Media Square, Plc. He is former Chairman of the magazine group Future, Plc.

Jeffrey Pfeffer is the Thomas D. Dee II Professor of Organizational Behavior at the Graduate School of Business, Stanford University.

Professor Pfeffer has taught at Stanford University since 1979. He is the author or coauthor of eleven books, including *The Human Equation: Building Profits by Putting People First*, *Managing with Power: Politics and Influence in Organizations*, *The Knowing-Doing Gap: How Smart Companies Turn Knowledge into Action*, and *Hidden Value: How Great Companies Achieve Extraordinary Results with Ordinary People*. His most recent book, *Hard Facts, Dangerous Half-Truths, and Total Nonsense: Profiting from Evidence-Based Management*, is coauthored with Robert Sutton.

Professor Pfeffer began his career at the Business School at the University of Illinois and then taught at the University of California, Berkeley. He has also been a visiting professor at the Harvard Business School.

He served on the board of Unicru, Inc. (acquired by Kronos, Inc. in August 2006). Currently serving on the board of directors of Audible Magic and SonoSite, Inc. (SONO), Professor Pfeffer consults to, and provides executive education for, numerous companies, associations, and universities in the United States. He also writes a monthly column on management issues titled *The Human Factor* for the business magazine *Business 2.0*.

Sir Gerry Robinson is the former Chairman of Allied Domecq, an international company that operated spirits and wine companies and quick-service restaurants.

After leaving college at age seventeen, Sir Gerry planned to become a priest. Instead, in 1965, he joined Matchbox Toys (a division of Mattel, Inc.), a company he stayed with for nine years before moving to Lex Service Group, Plc.

In 1980 he joined Grand Metropolitan as the Finance Director of the U.K. Coca-Cola business. He became Managing Director in 1982 and then took up the mantle of CEO of Grand Met's Contract Services Division. In 1987 he led the management buyout of the business from Grand Metropolitan.

He joined Granada, Plc. as CEO in 1991, latterly overseeing the company's takeover of Forte Hotels in 1996. He was then instrumental in the merger between Granada Group and Compass Group, Plc. in 2000. He retired from Granada in 2001 and became Chairman of Allied Domecq, Plc. a year later. He stood down as Chairman after a takeover by Pernod Ricard.

About the Contributors

Currently Sir Gerry is Chairman of Moto Hospitality Ltd., the United Kingdom's leading operator of motorway service areas.

Sir Nick Scheele is currently Chancellor at the University of Warwick, a position he accepted in October 2001.

Prior to that Sir Nick, a thirty-eight-year veteran of Ford Motor Company, retired in 2005 as President and member of the Board of Directors.

His work with Ford began in 1966, working in Purchasing, Supply and Procurement in Britain. Twenty years later, he was president of Ford, Mexico, where he directed manufacturing and marketing operations.

In 1992 he returned to Britain as Vice Chairman of Jaguar Cars, quickly rising to become Chairman and CEO. During his seven years with Jaguar, sales doubled and Jaguar regained its place as one of the world's leaders in terms of brand image, product quality, and customer satisfaction.

In July 2000 he became President of Ford Europe, and is credited with having directed the increasingly successful transformation of Ford's European business. In October 2001 he was appointed President and COO of Ford's global operations as well as a member of its board of directors.

Sir Nick was awarded his knighthood in 2001.

Ivan Seidenberg is Chairman of the Board and CEO of the premier network company Verizon.

About the Contributors

Mr. Seidenberg was instrumental in forming Verizon through a number of mergers and acquisitions. He has led Verizon since its inception, first as co-CEO in 2000, then as sole CEO since 2002, and as Chairman since 2004.

Prior to the creation of Verizon, Mr. Seidenberg was Chairman and CEO of Bell Atlantic and NYNEX. He began his communications career more than forty years ago as a cable splicer's assistant and has held numerous operations and engineering assignments, including various leadership positions at NYNEX and Bell Atlantic.

In 2007 President George W. Bush named Mr. Seidenberg to the National Security Telecommunications Advisory Committee, which advises the president on communications issues related to national security, emergency preparedness, and the protection of critical infrastructure.

Mr. Seidenberg also serves as Director of Honeywell, Inc.; the Museum of Television and Radio; The New York Hall of Science; Pace University; Verizon Foundation; and Wyeth.

John Stewart was Director at McKinsey & Company for forty years, specializing in solving problems for technological organizations.

During this time, he worked in several highly technical industries such as aerospace, electronics, and pharmaceuticals. In addition he has worked in several manufacturing industries, including automotive, steel, chemicals, and paper.

About the Contributors

Mr. Stewart's concentration has been on strategic issues facing these industries, their need to improve operating performance, and the organizational change needed to implement revised strategies or new operational programs. He is now retired.

⊰ ACKNOWLEDGMENTS ⊱

First and foremost, a heartfelt thanks goes to all of the executives who have candidly shared their hard-earned experience and battle-tested insights for the Lessons Learned series.

Angelia Herrin at Harvard Business School Publishing consistently offered unwavering support, good humor, and counsel from the inception of this ambitious project.

Brian Surette, Hollis Heimbouch, and David Goehring provided invaluable editorial direction, perspective, and encouragement. Much appreciation goes to Jennifer Lynn for her research and diligent attention to detail. Many thanks to the entire HBSP team of designers, copy editors, and marketing professionals who helped bring this series to life.

Finally, thanks to our fellow cofounder James MacKinnon and the entire Fifty

Acknowledgments

Lessons team for the tremendous amount of time, effort, and steadfast support for this project.

—Adam Sodowick
   Andy Hasoon
   Directors and Cofounders
   Fifty Lessons